PRESENT CONDITIONS

ALSO BY JOSEPH MASSEY

Full-length books

Illocality
To Keep Time
At the Point
Areas of Fog

Chapbooks

Minima St.
Eureka Slough
Bramble
Property Line
Out of Light
Within Hours
The Lack Of
Exit North
Thaw Compass
An Interim
What Follows
5 Poems

PRESENT CONDITIONS

A Chapbook

Joseph Massey

Hollyridge Press
Venice, California

Hollyridge Press
P.O. Box 2872
Venice, California 90294
www.hollyridgepress.com

Cover and Book Design by Rio Smyth
Cover Image and Author Photo by Joseph Massey

Manufactured in the United States of America by Lightning Source

ISBN-13: 978-1-7325133-0-3
ISBN-10: 1-73251-330-9

"Present Conditions," "Without," and "Nashawannuck" first appeared
as broadsides from Tungsten Press. Many thanks to Wolfram Swets.

"Garden Level" first appeared in *The Cossack Review* and *Dreamstreets*.

"Notes on a Dead End" and "Between Seasons" first appeared
in *GeoHumanities*, the journal of the American Association of Geographers.

25 24 23 22 21 20 19 18   10 9 8 7 6 5 4 3 2 1

Contents

Present Conditions

PRESENT CONDITIONS

Today the weather within
is the weather without.
Even the wind is broken,
stammering over gnarled stalks
and black bulbs punctured through
snowpack. I'm alive
in the contrast, dragging myself
from a dream, eyes adjusting
to the light. In a semaphore
of stripped limbs
the sun, segmented, multiplies.

NOTES ON A DEAD END

Words won't cohere
around an echo's
leftover pulse:
a car alarm
gone quiet

in an otherwise barren
parking lot at dusk—

barren but for an aura
levitating a dumpster;

asphalt softened
into orange; dead
leaves crushed,
dim confetti.

Gravel, mud,
filthy slush—
there isn't a phrase
to be found here.

A tangle of names
gaze blank
through blank cold.

AMULET (MIDWINTER)

i.

All day rain returns snow
to lawn and asphalt.

Potholes mirror
the low sky's
dead eye—

gray glare
without variation
in a variable wind.

ii.

Iced-over branches graph
the oncoming gloam;

the deepening blue

I mistook for dawn
drawn between overlapping lines.

iii.

A ritual silence dissolves night
into day, ballasts me
to the room

bludgeoned
by winter's nothing.

iv.

Traffic's shadow wobbles
on the far wall. In the window

a garland of late gulls struggle
to cleave a shape from the cold.

NASHAWANNUCK

All ice, the pond is rough
with half-sunk sticks,
branches, a past season's detritus.

The mangled calligraphy
made legible
by a gathering silence. Now snow

sweeps out across the pond
aligned with a field
aligned with a cemetery, seamless—

seamless
as though a world
were there to be unwritten.

GARDEN LEVEL

i.

Night gives nothing back; it only appears to cohere. The patterns dissolve without pause. An animal rattles mulch and twice-dead leaves piled against the window. I know the walls are there for the sounds they sift into the room—the room that inhabits me—underground.

ii.

Sun in the shape of a quadrangle on a wood floor. Cur-
tains blown horizontal split it in half. Dust divots air,
dents the pale afternoon. An hour isn't like anything,
not even itself. A window, a patch of lawn, a street for
the tide of its noise, for measure. A stream of particulars
undoing the room.

iii.

It can take all day to filter out the debris of a dream, to see a thing contained by its terms. Call it clarity. You have to almost stop thinking; get up to the edge of the clanging at the back of the brain. Go dumb to the light.

iv.

Three weeks in and the season begins to click. Weather to word; word to weather. A bird circles, punctuates a bloodless sky—the husk we're under. The street a mono-chrome stream. Cold enough to numb thought.

v.

Snow light at dusk, the deepening bruise; a blue that hums. A soundless ringing between the eyes where all things sink and disperse. For once we're reading the world without the names by which we dream it. Nothing to say; nothing saying us.

vi.

Everything comes to a point along the horizon; every limb stripped to a line. Even the clouds sharpen, shaved against a mountain. A pond duplicates the scene—if your gaze drops. To suspend the senses in the drone of geometry. To forget the traffic here.

vii.

The way the mind bends to receive injured weather, the sudden warmth, as though half awake and watching a place—a room, a field—assemble itself one object at a time. A syntax expanding beneath fanned rays of gaping sun. Center everywhere, circumference nowhere.

MARCH, CLOSER

Around the edges the gleam
deepens, you'll see it—
the sting of it—

if you look long enough.
A new season bends

and bleeds through
what was wild.
The field

illegible
with language.

We're surrounded

by an exhaustion
of green
gouged out

by gray,
and a pothole
full of melted ice

reassembling sky.

PORTAL

Second day
of spring
and winter stilts
the signal: snow
in truncated gusts
performs its math
over what
the window
frames. Lines
between lawn
and sidewalk
fade; hedges
heavy, dusted,
heave into
wind, white
and whiter now,
a peripheral
blur, as I turn
in my chair
between stacks
of unread books.
Basement apartment—
grass stubble
claws at glass,
pockets
of darkness
other weather
won't reach.
I live to find
the language in

insect-pocked
soil, fast food
trash scattered
by a raccoon,
the vibration
of a passing
plow. Almost
underground,
time uncoils
without shadow's
measure, and
I leave
my clock
unplugged.
I live to see
particulars decay
and to graph them
with breath
and the sound
I send
through breath.

VIGIL

A contrail arcs
over the wreck. Snowbanks
returned to gravel; litter
and its language
ground to grit. This excuse
for spring. Nothing to see
beyond a blind spot
collapsing into afterimage.
Nothing to hear beyond a voice
consuming itself in an alley.
How the world expands
as a thought expands
with the angle of the season.
Between parking block
and dumpster
crocuses clarify
their square of shade.

CLEAR

After eight days of rain
what isn't overwritten
under sun. These

asphalt cracks
pushed further apart.
Eight days without

definition: gray walled
the room in, and I
thought I found a way

to stop thinking—to allow
gray to become a sound
I couldn't hum myself out of.

All I heard was a window.
A long weed beat
unevenly against it.

FOR A FAILED SUICIDE

How many days
since I last left my body.

Spring happened
but I didn't notice,

caught in an echo
that refused
to unremember.

I thought
I'd die to stop thinking.

I woke
in a locked ward.

My mind grazed
on a grid:

windows enforced
with wire mesh.
I knew I wasn't dead

when the colors came back.

Green hills
underscored
by cold linoleum.

FIFTH FLOOR

No one's walking
the hall. The ghost of a code
clings to a chalkboard
on a beige wall. Fluorescent
light vibrates my eyes.

This is what counts for silence.
The building's gills
breathing out.

Even the old man mumbling
the same fractured phrase
without pause
into a paper cup
becomes a kind of white noise.

Behind him
tinted windows
turn a world to winter.

CALLED BACK

I'm still a body
after a season spent

dying to leave it.
Was it winter

or spring, or the weeks
when they blend—

a sub-season
of mud, puddles

that froze overnight
and the next day,

half-melted, spiked
the sky's reflection.

ABOVEGROUND

The weather is the poem
that writes itself
unceasingly.

The bright unreal.

These shadows I hang
the hours on.

The wind carries

grass and gasoline,
manure and petrichor.

The psychedelia
of a flowering pear tree.

Look up through its branches:

white striations
blaring blue

after how many Mondays
immersed in sepia
and snow.

THESE DAYS

i.

Hungover, I watch wind compose a world too bright to comprehend: sidewalk scabbed with rocksalt, thick shadow thrashed thin through traffic. From this angle the road's a knot gone slack. I wait to cross while gulls shuffle north over a closed Chinese restaurant—the worn white sign and worn white wings, an unfinished phrase dissolving in air.

ii.

I spent the afternoon sifting through a dream—bright
rubble of syllables—for a voice to counter the rain.

iii.

These days are faceless. The hours monochrome. I talk
to myself, as I'm talking now, to drown the sound of
thought, to claim a space where absence hums—where I
become breathless, and you are all that's left.

ONE MONTH LATER

My mouth still moves
around language

that baffles me alive.
My vision blurs

but wherever I look
a world wakes.

I sit for hours
chanting in silence

the name of each thing
attached to each shadow

waving slowly
over white stucco.

PLEIN AIR

Forsythia
flood my vision—

the yellow world
flashing caution.

BETWEEN SEASONS

Morning dilates
a window
flanked by an unkempt hedge.

June arrived and the glare
grew particulate—thick

with gnats
collapsing
around the frame.

I've been indoors
for weeks, but old glass

warps the seam. Shade
spills over concrete;

clover packs a long fracture.

I'm grounded in these images

that slip
past the screen.

A chamber where a voice
throws itself in silence

and silence returns
at the edge of a word.

ON THE SOLSTICE

Heat lightning
stilts the gloam

and lingers
in the inner-eye.

This negotiation
between stasis
and abrasion,

honeysuckle
and car exhaust.

I move through
the room

or the room
moves through me

while night draws back
into insect static.

Air too thick to think

and the moon in a pool
on stained linoleum.

MAIN ST.

A passing siren
abbreviates panic,
removes me from thinking's
constant throb. Yellowjackets
carve a circular blur
around a soda can
standing in
pissed-on woodchips.
Nostalgia wanes
when it's this hot, when speech
contracts to half a breath
behind a word that won't come.
So humid
even the concrete wilts.

THE PRACTICE

Panic, the speechless
hour, blooms
in dust—

a spent web
vibrating
a corner.

Where am I
without a word
to hold against
the day,

to witness
transparency
as prayer
and ballast.

Afternoon dark
as late dusk.
I listen
to thunder

hollow
the particular
silence of hail

raining
against glass.

My mind
finally removed
from the room

dissolves
in outside sound.

WITHOUT

Sunday is dust
revolving
through slit curtains.

A blank page
bright as an ambulance
churning the humidity.

I've waited hours now

for the walls to recede,
for dusk.

For the windows
to go blind.

www.ingramcontent.com/pod-product-compliance
Lightning Source LLC
Chambersburg PA
CBHW030031290326
41934CB00005B/574